A Pile of

Giggles 2

~ Clean Acronyms, Puns, and One-Liners...For Teens and Their Families~

Success Families

Emma, Isaac, Hanna and SherLynne Beach

A Pile of Giggles 1 - Clean Acronyms, Puns, and One-Liners...For Teens and Their Families
Emma, Isaac, Hanna and SherLynne Beach, Success Families
Family Joke Books Series

ISBN-13: 978-1519778574
ISBN-10: 1519778570

.....

Dedication

To Ben B.
Enjoy!

Introduction

"Puns are the highest form of literature."
— *Alfred Hitchcock*

"Wit and puns aren't just decor in the mind; they're essential signs that the mind knows it's on, recognizes its own software, can spot the bugs in its own program."
— *Adam Gopnik*

***

We love puns, jokes and silly thoughts. Everything in this book is clean, silly, and perfect for young teens and their families to tell over and over.

Illustrated by children and a mom, this book inspires drawing fun conclusions about each joke.... So here's an idea...grab a cup of milk and a plate of cookies, a drawing pad of paper and some pencils, and see what your imagination comes up with as each pun and joke is shared.

Acronyms

Acronyms for the word "**A.C.R.O.N.Y.M.**":

- Alphabetical Code for Remembering Odd Names You Make up
- A Coded Rendition Of Names Yielding Meaning
- A Contrived Reduction Of Nouns, Yielding Mnemonics
- Another Cryptic Rendition Of Nomenclature You Memorize

A.D.D. = Americans For Donald Duck

A.D.I.D.A.S. = All Day I Dream About Soccer

A.O.L. = Anti On-Line

A.R.M.Y. = Ain't a Real Marine Yet

B.I.N.G. = Bing Is Not Google

B.M.W. = Bring Mechanic With!

B.O.S.S. = Built On Self Success

B.U.I.C.K. = Big Ugly Indestructible Compact Killer

C.D.-R.O.M. = Consumer Device, Rendered Obsolete in Months

C.O.M.P.U.T.E.R. = Capable Of Making Perfectly Uncomplicated Tasks Extremely Rigorous

D.E.N.I.A.L.= Don't Even Know I Am Lying

D.I.E.T. = Did I Eat That?

D.U.H. = Don't Understand, Huh?

F.L.U. = Fluids Leaking Unstoppably

F.O.R.D. = First On Race Day (thanks to Jack Peltzel)

G.R.E.A.T. = Get Really Excited About Today

H.O.N.D.A. = Hold On, Not Done Accelerating!

H.O.P.E. = Hold On, Pain Ends

I.D.G.A.F.= I Don't Give Away Food

L.A.M.E. = Laughable And Mildly Entertaining

L.I.F.E. = Learning Is Fun & Exciting

L.I.F.E. = Living It Fully Everyday!

L.I.S.P. = Lots of Infuriating & Silly Parentheses

L.I.V.E. = Learning Important Values Everyday

M.C.D.O.N.A.L.D. = Making Children Diners Order Nuggets And Large Drinks

N.A.S.C.A.R. = Non-Athletic Sport Centered Around Rednecks

P.O.T.S. = Plain Old Telephone System

S.A.L.T. = Same As Last Time

S.P.A.M. = Seriously, Poor Advertising Method!

S.U.B.A.R.U. = Still Usable, But All Rusty Underneath

T.E.A.M. = Together Everyone Achieves More

T.H.O.R. = The Hammer's Over Rated

T.W.I.T.T.E.R. = Things Which I Type That Everyone Reads

V.O.L.V.O. = Very Odd Looking Vehicular Object

W.A.T.E.R. = Wonderful And Totally Energizing Refreshment

W.E.I.R.D.= Wonderful Exciting Interesting Real Different

W.I.I.F.M. = What's In It For Me?

W.I.N.D.O.W.S. = Wonderful Interface No Dos User Would Sanction

PUNS

"But the helmet had gold decoration, and the bespoke armorers had made a new gleaming breastplate with useless gold ornamentation on it. Sam Vimes felt like a class traitor every time he wore it. He hated being thought of as one of those people that wore stupid ornamental armor. It was gilt by association."

— Terry Pratchett

A bicycle can't stand alone because it is two-tired.

Time flies like an arrow. Fruit flies like a banana.

They're selling dead batteries, free of charge.

Conjunctivitis.com is a site for sore eyes.

The best way to communicate with a fish is to drop them a line.

The cannibals ate the missionary and got a taste of religion.

I went to the Cashew factory last night. It was nuts!

He bought a donkey because he thought he might get a kick out of it.

Beware of alphabet grenades. If one of them goes off, it could spell disaster.

The horse got run over by a car. It's now in stable condition.

Her boyfriend had a wooden leg, until she broke it off.

He wears glasses during math because it improves division.

Becoming a vegetarian is a huge missed steak.

I once played the back end of a wasp in a pantomime play. But I thought I was the bees' knees...

The store promised a free abacus with a purchase, but I wouldn't count on it.

I wasn't very good at math till I put 2+2 together.

I went looking in the shops to buy a jack in a box but none jumped out at me

There are lots of people who are self aware. You know who you are

A backwards poet writes inverse.

Did you hear about the guy whose whole left side was cut off? He's all right now.

When the smog lifts in Los Angeles, U C L A.

It was an emotional wedding. Even the cake was in tiers.

I entered ten puns in a contest, and I thought I would win, but unfortunately, no pun in ten did.

When the waiter spilled a drink on his shirt, he said, "This one is on me."

I went to the butcher's the other day and I bet him 50 bucks that he couldn't reach the meat off the top shelf. He said, "No, the steaks are too high."

Snoring comes easily to me, in fact I can do it in my sleep

The police think the murder weapon may have been a colander, but that theory doesn't hold water

I took a poll recently and 100% of people were annoyed that their tent had fallen down.

I have a group of friends that go to restaurants to sample the food. They're my taste buds

I was having a dream and this voice said "on your marks, get set, go" and I woke with a start

I'm fed up with my landlord. He's always walking about like he owns the place

When I was younger I used to walk the plank. I couldn't afford a dog

I've never played Battleships B4. That joke's a bit hit or miss

Advent calendars-their days are numbered

Velcro: what a rip off

The past present and future walk into a restaurant. It was tense.

When a new hive is done bees have a house swarming party.

She got fired from the hot dog stand for putting her hair in a bun.

Pencils could be made with erasers at both ends, but what would be the point?

I relish the fact that you've mustard the strength to ketchup to me.

He didn't tell his mother that he ate some glue. His lips were sealed.

Even though the river has a bed, it won't stop running.

When Peter Pan punches, they Neverland.

Let's talk about rights and lefts. You're right, so I left.

When a clock is hungry it goes back four seconds.

A boiled egg every morning is hard to beat.

I went to buy some camouflage trousers yesterday but couldn't find any.

I've been to the dentist many times so I know the drill.

Two fish are in a tank. One says to the other, "Err...so how do you drive this thing?"

Without geometry, life is pointless.

A chicken crossing the road is truly poultry in motion.

Being struck by lightning is a shocking experience!

The roundest knight at King Arthur's table was Sir Cumference. He acquired his size from far too much pi.

I went to a seafood disco last week....and pulled a mussel.

She had a photographic memory but never developed it.

Two antennas met on a roof, fell in love and got married. The ceremony wasn't much, but the reception was brilliant!

In democracy it's your vote that counts; in feudalism it's your count that votes.

I know, this pun isn't very punny. It isn't very punny now is it?

I used to think I was indecisive, but now I'm not so sure.

Never trust an Atom. They make up everything.

I wanted to be a butcher but I didn't make the cut.

Exit signs, they're on the way out.

I've never played Battleships B4. That joke's a bit hit or miss

An astronaut broke the law of gravity and earned a suspended sentence

That was a poor joke about infinity – it didn't have an ending

A man just assaulted me with milk, cream and butter. How dairy.

The other day I held the door open for a clown. I thought it was a nice jester.

I did a theatrical performance about puns. Really it was just a play on words.

In the winter my dog wears his coat, but in the summer he wears his coat and pants.

Energizer Bunny arrested -- charged with battery.

The chicken crossed the playground to get to the other slide.

The best way to stop a charging bull is to take away his credit card.

The marine biology seminars weren't for entertainment, but were created for educational porpoises.

Show me a piano falling down a mineshaft and I'll show you A-flat minor.

England doesn't have a kidney bank, but it does have a Liverpool

They just found a sword swallower dead. The police suspect it's an inside job.

The man who fell into an upholstery machine is fully recovered.

I used to have a fear of hurdles, but I got over it.

Yesterday I accidentally swallowed some food coloring. The doctor says I'm OK, but I feel like I've dyed a little inside.

A skunk fell in the river and stank to the bottom.

A new type of broom came out, it is sweeping the nation.

My neighbor is in the Guinness World Records. He has had 44 concussions. He lives very close to me. A stone's throw away, in fact.

The man who survived mustard gas and pepper spray is now a seasoned veteran.

I don't trust these stairs because they're always up to something.

The shoemaker did not deny his apprentice anything he needed. He gave his awl.

When William joined the army he disliked the phrase 'fire at will'.

Need an ark to save two of every animal? I noah guy.

A prisoner's favorite punctuation mark is the period. It marks the end of his sentence.

I think Santa has riverfront property in Brazil. All our presents came from Amazon this year.

He drove his expensive car into a tree and found out how the Mercedes bends.

Police were called to a daycare where a three-year-old was resisting a rest.

I couldn't quite remember how to throw a boomerang, but eventually it came back to me.

I'm reading a book about anti-gravity. It's impossible to put down.

My friend's bakery burned down last night.
Now his business is toast.

I'm glad I know sign language, it's pretty
handy.

I'd tell you a chemistry joke but I know I
wouldn't get a reaction.

I wasn't originally going to get a brain transplant, but then I changed my mind.

I used to be a banker but I lost interest.

A friend of mine tried to annoy me with bird puns, but I soon realized that toucan play at that game.

You feel stuck with your debt if you can't budge it.

Local Area Network in Australia: the LAN down under.

He often broke into song because he couldn't find the key.

Every calendar's days are numbered.

He had a photographic memory which was never developed.

A plateau is a high form of flattery.

The short fortune teller who escaped from prison was a small medium at large.

Those who get too big for their britches will be exposed in the end.

When you've seen one shopping center you've seen a mall.

Bakers trade bread recipes on a knead to know basis.

Acupuncture is a jab well done.

Marathon runners with bad footwear suffer the agony of defeat.

When an actress saw her first strands of gray hair she thought she'd dye.

A pessimist's blood type is b-negative.

I used to work in a blanket factory, but it folded.

Corduroy pillows are making headlines.

Sea captains don't like crew cuts.

Does the name Pavlov ring a bell?

A gossip is someone with a sense of rumor.

Without geometry, life is pointless.

When you dream in color, it's a pigment of your imagination.

Reading while sunbathing makes you well-red.

When two egotists meet, it's an I for an I.

I'm getting a little Chile up here.

Going back and forth like this, we're always Russian.

There was this woman named Tina who was killed in this horrible accident when one of the golden arches at a McDonald's fell on her and it was an arch-on-Tina (Argentina).

I feel myself fading away I feel like I'm going into a France.

And where all the fish go on vacation: Finland.

Biology-whiz that was a good one.

I chem do this all day.

The yolks on you.

I asked a horse if he had a dollar. He said "no, but I have fore quarters."

My wife's here, she's a real sweet tea.

Look, if you don't like it, the exodus over there.

No more nouns, I'm proverbs.

I'm gonna make like John the Baptist and skip ahead, because I think I'm doing a good job. That psalms it up.

The fattest knight at King Arthur's round table was Sir Cumference. He acquired his size from too much pi.

I thought I saw an eye doctor on an Alaskan island, but it turned out to be an optical Aleutian.

A rubber band pistol was confiscated from algebra class, because it was a weapon of math disruption.

No matter how much you push the envelope, it'll still be stationery.

A dog gave birth to puppies near the road and was cited for littering.

A grenade thrown into a kitchen in France would result in Linoleum Blownapart.

Two silk worms had a race. They ended up in a tie.

Atheism is a non-prophet organization.

Two hats were hanging on a hat rack in the hallway. One hat said to the other: "You stay here. I'll go on a head."

 I wondered why the baseball kept getting bigger. Then it hit me.

The midget fortune-teller who escaped from prison was a small medium at large.

The soldier who survived mustard gas and pepper spray is now a seasoned veteran.

Two Eskimos sitting in a kayak were chilly, so they lit a fire in the craft. Unsurprisingly it sank, proving once again that you can't have your kayak and heat it too.

Always trust a glue salesman. They tend to stick to their word.

The butcher backed up into the meat grinder and got a little behind in his work.

The one who invented the door knocker got a No-bell prize.

The experienced carpenter really nailed it, but the new guy screwed everything up.

The girl quit her job at the doughnut factory because she was fed up with the hole business.

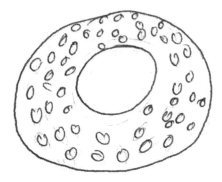

I like European food so I decided to Russia over there because I was Hungary. After Czech'ing the menu I ordered Turkey. When I was Finnished I told the waiter 'Spain good but there is Norway I could eat another bite'.

The first time I used an elevator it was really uplifting, then it let me down.

There was once a cross-eyed teacher who couldn't control her pupils.

I relish the fact that you've mustard the strength to ketchup to me.

Atheists don't solve exponential equations because they don't believe in higher powers.

When the cannibal showed up late to the luncheon, they gave him the cold shoulder.

I was going to look for my missing watch, but I could never find the time.

Don't trust people that do acupuncture, they're back stabbers.

Novice pirates make terrible singers because they can't hit the high seas.

I took a picture of a field of wheat, it was grainy.

Claustrophobic people are more productive thinking outside the box.

I once heard a joke about amnesia, but I forgot how it goes.

I was going to buy a book on phobias, but I was afraid it wouldn't help me.

Smaller babies may be delivered by stork but the heavier ones need a crane.

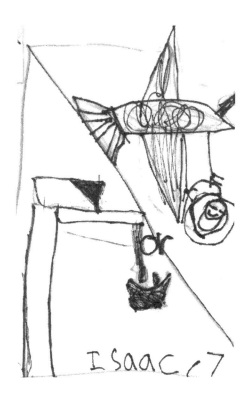

Some people's noses and feet are built backwards: their feet smell and their noses run.

Sleeping comes so naturally to me, I could do it with my eyes closed.

If towels could tell jokes they would probably have a dry sense of humor.

I heard the new auto body shop that opened comes highly wreck-a-mended.

John Deere's manure spreader is the only equipment the company won't stand behind.

Jill broke her finger today, but on the other hand she was completely fine.

I was struggling to figure out how lightning works then it struck me.

I really wanted a camouflage shirt, but I couldn't find one.

My new theory on inertia doesn't seem to be gaining momentum.

There was a big paddle sale at the boat store. It was quite an oar deal.

Broken puppets for sale. No strings attached.

Einstein developed a theory about space, and it was about time too.

Two peanuts were walking in a tough neighborhood and one of them was a-salted.

The magician got so mad he pulled his hare out.

My tailor is happy to make a pair of pants for me, or at least sew it seams.

I try wearing tight jeans, but I can never pull it off.

My daughter asked me if I was having fun doing the laundry. I replied, 'Loads.'

People are choosing cremation over traditional burial. It shows that they are thinking out of the box.

If you don't pay your exorcist you get repossessed.

More Fun

New and Improved Names for Boring
Everyday Things

Couch = People Shelf

Books = Manual Films

Bracelets = Clockless Watches

Air Horn = Spray Scream

Bottled Water = Snowman Blood

Feather = Bird Leaf

Other funny words...

Crick: The sound that a Japanese camera makes.

Dockyard: A physician's garden.

Khakis: What you need to start the car in Boston .

Oboe: An English tramp.

Pasteurize: Too far to see.

Propaganda: A gentlemanly goose.

Toboggan: Why we go to an auction.

One-Liners

How did I escape Iraq? Iran.

I can't believe I got fired from the calendar factory. All I did was take a day off.

I wanna make a joke about sodium, but Na..

My first job was working in an orange juice factory, but I got canned: couldn't concentrate.

What was Forrest Gump's email password? "1forrest1"

Life is all about perspective. The sinking of the Titanic was a miracle to the lobsters in the ship's kitchen.

Sorry, my dog ate your text message.

I changed my password to "incorrect". So whenever I forget what it is the computer will say "Your password is incorrect".

When I call a family meeting I turn off the house wifi and wait for them all to come running.

Apparently I snore so loudly that it scares everyone in the car I'm driving.

Going to church doesn't make you a Christian any more than standing in a garage makes you a car.

I work to buy a car to go to work.

My kid had her driver's test the other day. She got 8 out of 10. The other 2 guys jumped clear.

I eat my tacos over a Tortilla. That way when stuff falls out, BOOM, another taco.

Turning vegan is a big missed steak.

"Could you take a couple steps back. I have a nut allergy."

One day you're the best thing since sliced bread. The next, you're toast.

Sources

http://abbreviations.yourdictionary.com/articles/funny-acronyms.html#vARysxOW4bPcV1dh.99

http://examples.yourdictionary.com/examples-of-puns-for-kids.html#oPRx8qU8dTesIZwD.99

http://iteslj.org/c/jokes-puns.html

http://mentalfloss.com/article/69463/50-amazing-puns-past-pun-competitions

http://onelinefun.com/puns/

http://punjokes.com/#sthash.lykbhZsi.dpuf

http://www.funenglishgames.com/funstuff/funnypuns.html

http://www.funny2.com/acronymsd.htm

http://www.funny2.com/punsb.htm

http://www.goodreads.com/quotes/tag/puns

http://www.jokes4us.com/peoplejokes/funnyacronyms.html

http://www.panix.com/~clp/humor/puns/Dumb_puns.html

http://www.punoftheday.com

http://www.rd.com/jokes/puns/

http://www.sliptalk.com

http://www.telegraph.co.uk/comedy/comedians/funniest-puns-in-history/

http://www.tnellen.com/cybereng/lit_terms/puns.html

More Available

By SherLynne Beach

and SuccessFamilies.com

- Powerful Mind: A class workbook for adults and children
- Mind Chatter Mastery Course
- Timeless Principles Of Raising Great Kids: Discover timeless wisdom, seemingly magical secrets to building strong families and a practical, ... best-selling authors & mentors
- Cursive Jokes Copywork 1: Write and Laugh!
- Manuscript Jokes Copywork 1: Write and Laugh
- Proverbs for Children: Handwriting, Copy-Work and Memorization (Volume 2)
- Simple Outlines Workbook: Trackable Progress K-3 Short Compositions Practice Workbook 1 of 3 (Writing Series).
- Simple Rough Drafts Workbook: Writing Steps Series, 2nd of 3 books (Volume 2)
- Simple Final Drafts Workbook: Trackable Progress K-3 Short Compositions Practice Workbook 2 of 3
- A Pile of Giggles 1, 2 and 3 (jokes and puns)

More SuccessFamilies
Books and Courses
Coming in 2016

- Silly Spelling Practice
- Thinking Through Books –Basic Reports (inspired by the Ben Carson Story)
- Classics Reading List –Pocket Book
- I AM in Charge Of My Mind Series, Journals and Workbooks and Courses
- I AM in Charge of my Emotions Series, Let Go and Heal Journals, Workbooks and Instruction
- Family Joke Books
- Children's Books
- And MORE!

Made in the USA
Middletown, DE
05 July 2017